sometimes, patience

sometimes, patience

poems by
Marija Leilynn

To the first, eager loved ones to seek my heart in and behind these words, and give grace enough so that I can step further toward the softness I so dearly long to embody. Thank you. Sincerely.

Contents

for the doubtful.

what i mean when i say healing

if i mistake
my darling obsessions
for love
and love like i know how,
let go like i know nothing,
promise me humility.
make of me mist
and pray i catch the light.
take these tears
for the fragrance of God
and rend this veil i fool with.
anoint these homeless kisses
into place and say to me
it's over now,
you're forgiven.

even to believe
i must touch wounds.

Inside the Night Drawer

Two unopened redivias pruned
out of bedrock and my ceramic
arm extended to give
to him.

A skipping stone
thumbed then fostered
in his pocket

for us and tomorrow, returning
home to rest with me
though my heartbeat ricochets

between the upswing
of my lungs and the plunge
back down. Beside him,

I dream of enduring—
a garden patient for affection,
the rippling surface which

always stills. But I wake
before morning and see
the open window,
I'm what's there

in the distance, black-mouthed hills
fouled by a spit of stars.

Before the Sowing

Touched by your goodness,

I am like a bracing
wisp of autumn air,

the rapture I allow

of every little death enduring until
touched by your goodness

I am like a moment

of forgetfulness, for the leaves
crumble when they collapse
upon the expectant skin of God

and I must forgive myself
for loving something back

to the way it came.

dating while abstinent.

I never lied. I spit the apple half-eaten to the grassless soil of earth,
pose like a modern exhibit haunting hunting ground. Human speak,

human here, so quiet a twig snaps, the stem from the core. I've eaten
nothing for dinner and all I could find is the leftovers of a premade

possibility. Orchard keepers lie, forbidden fruit poison to my flesh if I
eat the skin. Made my bed in the juice of it. Thought it like

a sweet dream, curled nose into white tuff beneath tail, counted the
leaping over those trees, pretend I'm not being chased. He never loved

me anyway, he's got a bow but cupid doesn't look like this. Trying to
make us lovers by hanging me in the butcher's window shopping for

venison, what a cute way to say I'm wanted. Slicing a heart through
the pulmonary. Something so rich about the color red applied to the

lips. Makes a man go crazy. The time dismantled by my doe gaze,
fixed, when I rarely stay enough to stand in opening. Fools' green, it's

fenced. The time, would you look at it? Where's the rabbit when you
need him. Where's the burrow these legs can wedge through, he said

they looked sexy today. Enough to make him hungry for the meat,
pure muscle. What's under but bone?

THE ARRIVAL

Coffee dark roasted then wasted,
spilt warping wood. It was sweet,
for a time. Marked my calender
for mid-May until an October
storm yanked your flight
back home. I'm the layover.
No longer a hello, a goodbye
that never leaves.
If I listen more than say and
stare more than see,
either way it's stranger.
I am the stranger.
I still know you in my head
when you're away. You knew
me before I began trying to let
being be like it was
but it's not
and we say goodbye now.
Don't look at me like that.
Look at me.
I just love you.

they tell me chapel is mandatory.

plumes of   light
through panes of stained
window glass /
members of us
believe the dust shimmers
like a choir of assurance.
others a fever.
others Hell.

that sultry shrine adores
half-truths. eternal damnation is
a state of being / the absence of anything
but longing of liberty,

a movement / rise please
be seated repeat
with perpendicular arms
to implanted wooden pews grit
ensnared in the teeth under
tight-lipped whispers
forgive my right hand *forgive me*
choking my left the way
folds crease the ironed skirt
laid on the duvet as jesus still waits
for his garments, pinned on the laundry line,
waiting while a child wails
no   no   they hate me there.
they don't hate you,
they don't know you.   exactly.

claim a sanctuary
here though its humming thick with
the sound of   Hell,
chanting blind though our eyes lock
enchanted by the flickering, fractured hues.

i will walk out
fire alarm breathless
behind me.   praying, pleading,   come.
maybe we will   wake.

her elopement

winter erases yesterday
colorless, the sun seducing us all
into shivering air.
following behind their holding hands,
i see the little breaths which i wove
into her braids, the white folds
of her blouse borrowed
hours before.
by march, the cold outlives its
innocence, weighs upon
our wildflowers. impatient
for august, we call the peeling birch
an altar. their vows, my aches
divorcing skin from spirit
like branches bare, tracing
across the sky.

she was all my time alone
until alone i became,
the wonder left in the footpaths
behind us, the memorials we write.
can i call this grief—
a loving i must make
of our thinning moments.

Where My Helplessness Goes

Inside your palm, clinging too tight
to confess my own pain.

To the cabin swearing prayer with
a basin of wishes eager for empathy.

Toward the night sky firing one rapid
flame after the next. Leaving me
below, wrinkling the soot.

And against my bruising spine, sounding
out your name through clenched teeth,
as if I hold half the bitten
white chocolate moon in my mouth,
melting by the heat of my hunger.

Beyond your vanity, there are wolves
that howl this way. Those who,
on their most starving night, whimper
at the last beacon left, coiling
their sliver bodies beside ivory wool
to keep warm until morning.

second kiss

vacancy has always meant
room for more and that road,
littered with dust and gravel,
drank my gasoline. in park
i knew language like heaven
laughing while
i reached for its body
gauzed in stolen lilies,
and asked why God couldn't
come sooner to save me.

after the first kiss, i cursed
profousley in disbelief
that my lips flowered
weakly then all at once
in the moonlight. that's
the way these gardens learn.
filling their mouths with the
light that blinds them. painting
their foreheads red with blood
and saying it's sacrificial to name
a wound a rose. since then i've
skinned myself raw against too many
sofas shoved underground just
wanting to unfold in the damp and
supple sod, then silenced the way
it made me weep,
like God did, even if by day
i'd debut anew, smooth-skinned
and well.

SEAMAID, TEMPEST BATHING

I bartered my deliverance for the contour of your puckered chin and
sent the ship back into the rage for tomorrow. It never came. We

waited with our bundled tinder bodies so close I could've curled one
flame of your hair tight around my ring finger. I never did.

I knew prayer like a seagull's gawk, like my blistered throat when I
pledged to bring God home to you, snap on your light in any bad

weather. The rain could thunder in and cheat me of rest and I'd still
fetch your cup of water in case you woke. In that hampered fantasy,

you're urgent for my nurturing. You sing me until our civilized misery
makes me happiest but in the speck of your eye the color of triton sin,

I'm rowboat wreckage necklacing all his lifesavers while I anchor my
faith on shore. Behind me hung God's only son like a sailor on the

splintered mast, cursing the sapphire swell of heaven until it wept too.
The saltwater leaked into my rotting trunks of treasure, my pirated

rations of time, and you drank it all, making us both thirsty, then asked
me to save you and that finished me. Is it finished now? This

outstretched framework, these futile confessions flared up if blood
thaws clear from the man between us?

Gospel of Fathers

1 He spoke to me, saying, "that's not the way to talk to your father." Why is he so defensive? He's not wrong but he's not right. [2]Jesus help me, talk to your Father. Who art in heaven, hollow is His name. [3]I just wanted to communicate, say something is wrong. Not be punished for it. Is there? A punishment? I don't know. That's the point, it's a plea for help. [4]I'm trying not to plea and ask instead, head bowed, reverent. I ask, but say, "so there's something I wanted to talk about," followed by everything. Watch your tone, young lady, and now we're shouting. Now I'm pleading by leaving for air. [5]I think I love him, [6]isn't it good to? When someone isn't gentle and doesn't say much and tries to control everyone, though occasionally comes in to kiss my forehead when I'm sleeping. He thinks [7]I don't notice. [8]My ex-boyfriend noticed. He used to kiss me on the forehead, call me a lovely little invention. Some kind of making up for the father-silence. [9]Invention, alright. All hardware and metal littering the floor, leftover shards of being [10]made in my father's image and if you're not careful I will harm you, slice right into that fragile skin. [11]You're the one that will stain. I'm the one God's bleeding hands are trying to shape.

2 Therefore, I consider asking my father if he wants tea when I see him cupless and needy on the living room couch. [2]I ask, then make it for him though he doesn't turn his head to say yes. Doesn't add the honey thank you,

so I swirl that sticky gold with the milk like this will, at last, be a holy offering. [3]Your will be done, father, here's your mug. Here's the love you expect: this labor. Is not love more than my understanding? [4]Lean not on your own understanding, give him the tea, acknowledge him, let him taste it. Taste and see you are not a child of the flesh but a [5]child of God. [6]What happens if he doesn't like the tea? He'll ask if it's made from the right water—did you use the tap? Did you put the filter on it like I asked? Here, let me do it. Why are you crying? Never mind just give me the kettle. Look what you did, spilled all over yourself, stupid child. [7]And if he says nothing, he'll take one sip then leave the cup for cold. Pretend to be reading. Pretend to be [8a]good, good father. It's who you are, who you are. On earth as it is in Heaven.

3 For this reason, I've felt justified to neglect. How else do I respond to his asking for my time? It's a waste? [2]Where's mother, she understands. You wouldn't believe the conversations we have. Poetry, verse, some sort of tongue-speak from the fruit of the vine, chalice full as we break the bread. [3]It tastes like communion, [4]like Jesus at the table saying come, as you are, all you who are weary. All you little children, this is my Father's house. [5]Lord, show me The Father. My momma says He's our Abba, intimacy deeper than the roots of her father, who left my grandmother working in the mines for her three children. [6]My momma took time to look to the heavens from a lava-rock island to [7]call God, Papa. Like a plea for help. A hope for healing. [8]An understanding that a plea is just an earnest prayer without fear of denial and all that's left is acceptance. [9]Where's my father in my prayers? [10]Still back at the healing, a small boy waiting for his father to kiss him on the forehead as he sleeps knowing he's never coming. [11]My father has become a father to my grandfather while sitting at his hospital bed. Telling him stories, telling me to visit. Tells us all, before it's too late, visit. [12]Forgive his vices and his shouting and kiss his thinning, leathery skin and sit with him. Just sit in that silence and let it soften all that wasn't there and find that this request is for my father, too. That I [13]listen, watch closely enough to see the sadness shadowing his face when thinking of his mistakes. I wish to hold him in those moments. I wish to lean my head on his shoulder and say thank you. [14]Thank you, father, for the ways you were there. For stumbling through the dark to bow over my tucked-in body and leave a forehead kiss, [15]trying your best not to wake me. Trying your best to be a good father. [16]I am your daughter, though we both are children, so I pronounce this word like a christening. And it's beginning to feel like an honest one. [17]Something like a promise.

In Oregon, By the Sea.

la mar // Spanish for "the sea"

To be kneeling beside the manner
of my name—
an endless, salty shade of blue.
How the thing
holds the land in its mouth,
laps its thousand tongues at each
shore / this rugged edge,
foaming hungry over porous basalt.

The glowing clementine sun
crowns eager at the Pacific's
spine, cooing, blushing the pale,
cloudless sky and light delights
in anything bearing it.

Lord,
to let there be
like your first word on the world.
To vault belonging, like water
from water, and believe this too
is good.

What My Longing Does
after Cecelia Llompart

Swell round, in
fanged cavern walls.

Infect me. Like the invisible
germ of a kiss.

Open the curtain window.

Taste like a pink tongue along
the bent cleft of an envelope.

Conch it through
the narrow glass neck of a bottle.

Carry it always between seam and skin.

Consider the tide.

Gargle salt, then sugar.

Like agave, flow sticky
from the core to the needle.

Unfold the minutes. Shawl them
loose about the birch.

SERPENT LAYERS

holy make this holy make this / eden in this pleasure / every bite
exposed / rots at the core / a false belief i was meant for / shedding
skin to dirt / weigh me by my girth / my flesh / seduced / with
flickering tongues like sweet damp ribbons / the color of

love / a knowing like / God

consider rippled muscle / alone asleep / God curving over broken
bone from the side of adam / God / taking me away / pronouncing my
name so / i listen / *maiden, wake* / i am / naked before you / *who told
you* / i told you / i sip
venom

             every

                    time

                          i'm alone.

LIVING ALONE IN DECEMBER

the nightlight far gone pale you hold finitude
close to your chest nails cinching the comforter
that fails to console against the shadows of
what source you can only name by morning. at
this point you plea for dreams. anything to fool
yourself into a chance of escaping what you try
but never succeed in adjusting to. the dark.

as little as asking accomplished you ask again
but to assure there is absence beneath the bed.
nothing but the dust which you came from. check
to be sure check after avoiding doesn't work it
never does you are your own shriveled phantom
caged by bone.

you can wake up now the demon says perching
at the bedpost dangling the unplugged bulb in
one claw and the two dull blades of your kitchen
shears in the other telling you practice, why
don't you, pry open those arms, and howl for
help if only the throat would loosen, but you're
so exhausted now that you're spelled by a stare,
body limp unable to hinge the smallest part of
yourself. muffled for a while, not sure if you
slept, you open your eyes to the branches pink by
dawn and still shaken, you make the bed.

CARCASS FOR MY ANGEL

"Isn't everything spiritual?" said my friend sipping
San Pellegrino with her toes damp in the mid-
May grass. This is just a frayed dimension and for
hope or hopelessness, neither one of us could say.
Only one week after, a ten-foot being bright as
polished brass was seen stooping into my passenger
seat, wings cramming against the margins of
my Subaru's interior. That afternoon I had been
raven-like, perched on the pickets enclosing what
I couldn't say, that these days, I am lying in a
spillage of my own fermented nectar. My ribs
sing open, nothing but a throbbing nest of muscle
left. Both prey and dark-winged, I know no rise,
only God knelt in the scraps of my becoming, and
driving home, the being pointed at the pearling sky
ripe enough to receive, to string together with the
webs in my palms.

REPENTANCE

I've wrung out my dignity and found my wrongs netted into the fibers
of what's left of me. Meals skipped to take better fruit from someone
else's labor;

thank you, too many times. I took it all, you see. The sticky flesh out
of hungry mouths. The nectar anoints my lips and colors them pinker
than the sky at dawn,

I'm a waking thing. A ceremony where my secrets lay open like
caskets, corpses pale and groomed. Death is stillness, the lake without
wind. Wake as a motor

slices the waters. Wake as cresting waves heave behind the lifted nose
of my get away to where no prejudice is preached to convict me.
I recite my own prayers

on Sunday morning, stumbling out. The path before me is fragile with
autumn, light flickering through the elms as if I could blow it out with
a wish, smoke

unfurling like Jesus never sacrificed himself in my place. I take
communion. Swallow his body and blood. I've consumed an entire
bottle of wine desperate

to know him. Does he stomach me? What if I call him Father? What if
I ask what glory means, in his own words? What of sin, if it makes me
wake. Wake

from my darkness.

SPELL THE DIM ABOVE

If this choice, then complete
disembodiment. Find me bent
beneath this insoluble sky
which has always appeared to mirror

the mind—a thousand borrowed
inventions doubting each other.

Where I've clung, the horizon drags
across in an infinite crease.
Its edge is the last sharp thing

before I'm carried away on a breath
let go, as if I know how. As if
I must for my upturned within
to abbreviate trust from mouthful
to savor.

Returning North in Spring

The Lord, the Lord,
such as the ground breaking
again and the milky
scent of its breathing.
The first song of a chickadee
nesting above our kitchen
window. The start of rain
and the song it too becomes
while safe in my mother's arms.

The Lord, the Lord,
such as my little hand
resting in hers, the same way
each sunlit day gives
the tulip its time.
Her soft fingertips climb
along my spine like a cluster of them
when I tremble, when some nerves
cinch, then go cold. Once,
in April's gray becoming, we went
walking to find the firstborn lilac.
Above it, a robin
reserved, and when we turned
for home, a mumbled chirr
rose from its throat.

breaking lessons

nothing beneath me is not
an alibi it's an apology.
no tricks, just concealed
solutions, wounds that don't
spare one bit of time.
promise, you can trust
me calling you love. what else
charges my pride
with doubt down to
the last evening, when the lone
wick withered by it's own light
while you hummed me
your favorite song. only now
i hear it in my chest, where,
if nothing else,
i'm softer now.

what friendship makes of me

each handful of sand is an impossible existence
and shores behold me. i leave craters there

with two bare feet like tiny attempts
to secure myself in uncertainty.

tide makes a home of them, and kneeling,
i sip welcomes with quivering hands.

regressing, the sea surrenders
it's thirst. i observe minutes further,

remembering. someday again, says
the horizon, so i stay staring, the brim
of us both nearly spilling tears.

UNDRESSING

Cursed is the soul I unsewed from the dress
I left unclasped as he left.

In love is never too far from the truth.

Lies are honest thoughts told in secret
and I carved every one into him in the shape
of a cross. Tattoos of my atonement. Pendants I'd
hang across my breast and pray he'd kiss and see it,
save himself from myself, from both of us
sipping blood.

I'd pour a glass and dine alone. My bread, my body,
broken into thirty pieces passed to the offering dish.
I'm not God. I repeated the lying truth, truthfully
repeat lies but by grace, through twenty-two years
terrified of intimacy, my heart turned
toward itself and saw the need
for nakedness

and it makes no sense but the wicked sense
of never being able to deserve love
again, again,
cured me.

WHEN I PRAY FOR YOU

One of us must be the left one.
One collapsed on the floor behind the wall
where the hushed music plays. To ache
for someone must mean admitting
everything in the mouth is acoustics.
Sounds I hate, sounds I love.
Everything pronounced is silence.
I manage that place. Make a home there,
invade nothing. Nothing, then came us
and we abandoned there, too. I'll wash our
remains with my hair, I beg

of God. If this liquored perfume tastes that
bitter I'd wait to be aquired as long
as it's definite. I don't want to linger I want
to last and most vows I make alone
stale between yes and no. I admit
I close by stuttering. My amen means
to pause for His presence forever, it's a sound
I hate and love. The low hum comes back
eventually and I'm still in the next room,
the left one, with the door shut and carpet
burning my bare knees.

HOMEMAKING

Consider, O Lord, how You pluck agates from shore, hold a pipe
in Your teeth   and make gray above me.

Consider each shored mineral swirling with artifact ripples, glazed
in Grandfather's basement,

marbled by the kitchen window as Grandmother hums alone.

The women, whose proverbs are stitched to their aprons, hemmed soft
to the laces
                consider the laces, clinging to their garden.

Consider my body, the pink conservatory of my skin, the webbed
furrows which trap every weak gust.

How, when unhinged,   I am of two birds,
both Yours.

Consider my lovers, each with an expiration sewed to his collarbone.
My gaping reservoir of desire
                drained easy before it's time.

Beloved awaiting, with his raw petalled heart, and Lord where
the groundwater surges forward,

there are hills between which fold me in half, each side better for it.

How I comb and comb that meadow for seedlings
to scoop up home for You,

but my offered hands are hourglassed, expecting the day
to break over me and scatter

that tobacco, cloud and flint, my little ones fishing next to their father.
I, with a handful of stones saying,   *consider this one.*

housekeeping

it's evening and you remember forgetting to load
laundry. you said you wouldn't do that, even
made a list but the sun is down now and studies
say you should sync sleep with the light or is it
with the dark either way you'll toss and sweat.
maybe you should try reading it could put your
mind at rest but you either dream or forget that
too while the moon watches over you with its
big glass eye. you know by now how carefully
God sets down the sun, hope-filled, a bit of color
slipping through the pines but most nights of late
anticipate difficultly waking with no coffee to
cure. can't sleep and can't wake. a cerebral war
between the left and the right, the head and the
heart, no weapons, just fists and words drawn
out of dusty pockets. just spitting ache down to
the territory line. you would do anything to be
emptied like the dryer after sixty minutes like
dishes after you move the sponge circuitously
while the sink sparkles as if to say you've done
well faithful servant forgive yourself for the mess
remember the monarch and the daisies you picked
by the pond the ones wedded to the pink peonies
there on your counter and what about the fawn
which did not flee when it saw you tip-toeing past
in her meadow of maiden grass but curled herself
to sleep, knowing you can, you will too.

upon asking if i'm afraid

less dagger more stained
glass with a riven portrait
of a blossom
more careful
like a fingerprint on
a dew kissed petal
and but the touch it takes
for every bead to ripen
into a river, drawn to
the sea you harbored into me,
graceful and sudden,
with every white-capped
wave heaved over the lull
of my vessel, and the
berthing place it was
to watch them varnish
my edges, softness like
a heap of drifting
to a hopeful again.

Find Marija Leilynn online:

Instagram: *@mar.lei.lynn*
Website: *www.marleilynn.com*
Email: *marijaleilynn@gmail.com*

Made in the USA
Monee, IL
01 June 2023

35119206R00023